THE COLLECTOR'S GUIDE TO NEW ART PHOTOGRAPHY VOL. 2

THE COLLECTOR'S GUIDE TO NEW ART PHOTOGRAPHY VOL. 2

EDITED BY AMANI OLU & JON FEINSTEIN

HUMBLE ARTS FOUNDATION

EDITED BY AMANI OLU & JON FEINSTEIN
PREFACE BY JON FEINSTEIN
INTRODUCTION BY VANESSA KRAMER
GRAPHIC DESIGN AND PRODUCTION BY AMANI OLU

First Edition
ISBN 978-0-9796425-1-7

Humble Arts Foundation
P.O. Box 1157
Old Chelsea Station
New York, NY 10113
(718) 928-9905
hello@hafny.org
hafny.org

To order in bulk call (718) 928-9905 or email hello@hafny.org

Printed and bound in Singapore by CS Graphics

Cover: David Benjamin Sherry, *Throwing Darts In Lovers Eyes*, 2010
Frontispiece: Kate Steciw, *Untitled*, 2010

Humble Arts Foundation is a non-profit committed to supporting and pro-moting new art photography. The New York-based organization serves the international art community by way of exhibition and publishing opportuni-ties, artists grants, and educational programming.

Founded in 2005 by amani olu and Jon Feinstein, Humble has been a pio-neering hub for showcasing new art photography, and has served as an international resource for collectors, galleries, museums, curators, photo editors, bloggers, and the public.

PREFACE

The past five years have witnessed a dramatic shift in various aspects of photography. Most superficially, digital technology has granted photographers, multimedia artists, and "the masses" the ability to create successful individual photographs with much greater ease than analog photography allowed previous generations. With the increasing democratization of the medium and the rampant absorption of the idea that "everyone is a photographer," artists looking to make their mark in the contemporary photographic canon are faced with a barrage of questions: How does one maintain one's individuality, voice, and artistic practice in an image-saturated, Internet-driven visual culture? How has Web-based culture accelerated artistic and photographic practice among younger generations? How does one distinguish between "emerging" and "amateur?" Does one's age define or contribute to intellectual or aesthetic freshness?

The Collector's Guide to New Art Photography is by no means a comprehensive survey of all that is currently happening in art photography. As evinced by the increasing number of collectives, blogs, online magazines, and "emerging photography" contests and competitions, it is nearly impossible to represent all the promising and intellectually engaging work that is surfacing now. Instead, this book contains a snapshot of a survey, pared down to 100 forward thinking photographers who we believe are pushing the medium into the future. In a landscape where far too many critics, academics, and art historians are declaring photography "over," our goal in publishing this book is to examine how photographers and photo-based artists are keeping the medium exciting, either in the ways they reference its history or in their attempts to distort or destroy it entirely.

The various styles of photography found in this book are nothing new on their own. That is to say, there is no representation or creation of an entirely new photographic "genre" per se. Process-based experimentation, representational portraiture, and staged, narrative-driven photography have existed in various forms since photography's inception, some works referring to art history or the history of photography, others attempting to break free and exist independent of its history. What we are most interested in with this collection, however, is what we see as a growing fusion or collapse of fixed photographic genres. Many of the photographers included transcend rigid categories and take a more fluid approach to image making—their work can no longer simply be limited to "conceptual," "documentary," or a variety of other descriptive, yet restrictive, classifications. With this second volume, now titled *The Collector's Guide to New Art Photography*, it has been our intention to create a tightly organized overview of what we see as the most promising photographic work being produced today.

JON FEINSTEIN
CO-FOUNDER AND CURATORIAL DIRECTOR
HUMBLE ARTS FOUNDATION

INTRODUCTION

For the second time, Humble Arts Foundation is introducing a diverse group of fresh and innovative emerging art photographers to the mainstream photography market. This is consistent with the foundation's modus operandi of discovering unknown talent and presenting it to collectors, curators, museum, gallery, and other art professionals. Meeting the needs of the broad-based clientele that makes up today's photography market, the book publishes an array of contemporary photographers whose interests range from technical experimentation with light to more conceptual approaches. These artists explore identity issues and a spectrum of topics related to current intellectual, cultural, artistic, and social discourse. In addition to a myriad of subjects, the book also includes a variety of scales, printing processes, and sources of inspiration.

It is always a thrill to discover new artists and respond to their work in unexpected ways. The selections here will undoubtedly evoke a wide range of reactions. For novice collectors, the book will offer an opportunity to view different photographic practices that can assist them with deciding on a genre of interest. In the case of seasoned collectors, it will serve as an update on the latest artists. In either circumstance, *The Collector's Guide to New Art Photography* functions similar to a Rorschach test with different images exercising a gravitational pull, summoning various ideas, thoughts, or memories. Perhaps you will reminisce about prom night after viewing Sarah Girner's image of a gown from decades past, or feel engulfed by a pleasant memory from a forgotten beach vacation upon seeing Paul Bobko's photographs of breaking waves. Daniel Coburn's photographs of models striking poses they find sexy make me smile. What viewers will surely walk away with is the undeniable power of the photographic medium.

The photographs presented in this volume are more accessible to the viewer than they might be in a gallery or museum setting. Among these great selections some stars twinkle bright. The market, however, as the last ten years have illustrated, can be capricious, and who among this new crop of talented photographers will stand the test of time is anyone's guess. Therefore, I warmly invite you, the viewer, to decide. It does not matter whether this is your first photography book or your one-thousandth. Your opinion matters as much as the next person's, and for that very reason, I urge you to trust your own intuition and believe in your own impeccable eye. I have learned that a genuine collector is not one who amasses photographs, but, rather, one who learns how to read them.

VANESSA KRAMER
WORLDWIDE HEAD OF PHOTOGRAPHS
PHILLIPS DE PURY & COMPANY

flat Death/sheet film (3), 2009, 9 x 12 in.

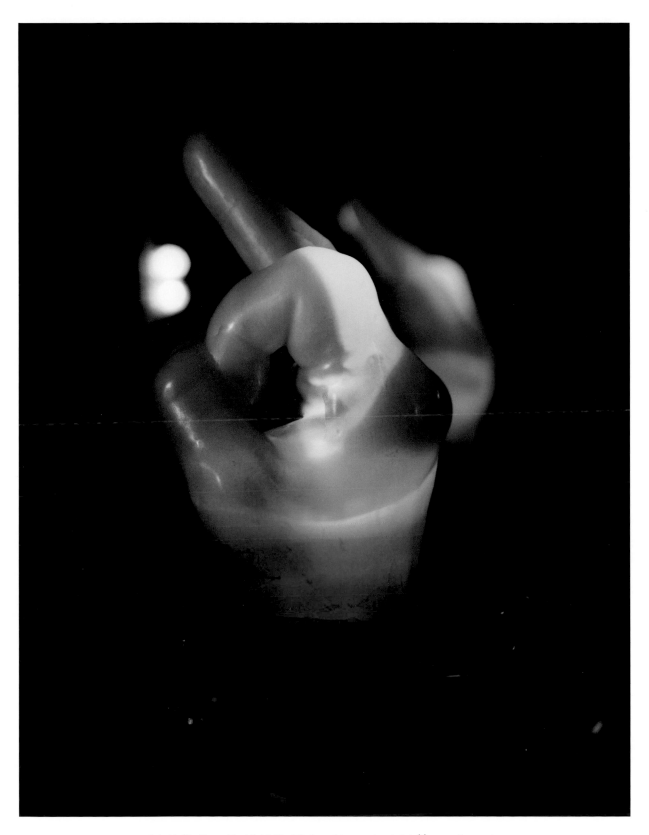

Ich Hoffe Dass Es Nicht Ein Weihnachtsgeschenk Ist (1), 2010, 8 x 10 in.

Gentleman #14, 2008, 11 x 17 in.

Gentleman #28, 2008, 16 x 20 in.

Untitled #18, 2010, 30 x 24 in.

Untitled #11, 2010, 30 x 24 in.

Caryl, 2009, 15.5 x 15.5 in.

ELIZABETH ATTERBURY

Seal Pool, 2010, 15.5 x 15.5 in.

Consolation, 2010, 42 x 52 x 12 in.

CLINT BACLAWSKI

The Titanic, Exodus, Motorola©, 2010, 42 x 52 x 12 in.

Untitled, 2009, 20 x 24 in.

Untitled, 2009, 20 x 24 in.

Civilian Joshua Osborne playing the role of an Iraqi civilian, Wadi Al–Sahara, Marine Corps Air Ground Combat Center, CA, 2008, 30 x 40 in.

Marines Sargent John Sexon, Lance Corporal Camerson Stark and Lance Corporal Joshua Stevens roleplaying as Taliban fighters, Marine Corps Mountain Warfare Training Center, CA, 2009, 30 x 40 in.

Exxon Mobil 9am to 11am, 2005, 90 x 110 cm.

Interest Income Comparison 4% – 8%, 2005, 90 x 110 cm.

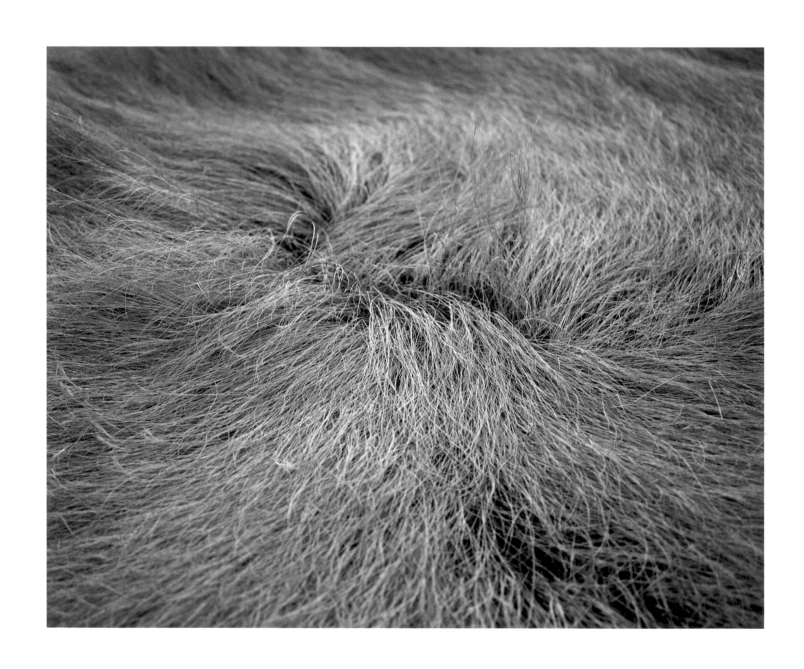

untitled #1, 2010, 24 x 20 in.

untitled #5, 2010, 24 x 20 in.

Mailboxes, Kolkata, India, 2007, 30 x 30 in.

Camper, Abel Tasman NP, New Zealand, 2008, 30 x 30 in.

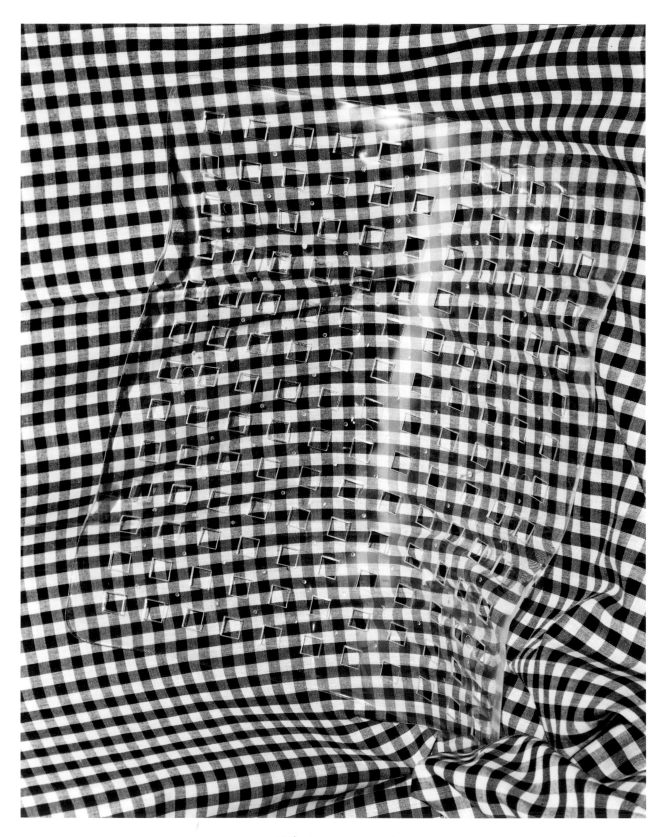

grid / grid, 2010, 40 x 30 in.

untitled (both yes and no), 2009, 24 x 20 in.

Untitled #5, 2005, 44 x 60 in.

Untitled #23, 2006, 44 x 60 in.

Ocean Wave 1, 2007, 20 x 26 in.

Ocean Wave 2, 2007, 20 x 26 in.

Daffodil flowers on color papers, 2010, Dimensions variable

Nuts on plate, 2010, Dimensions variable

Heath, 2005, 63 x 49 in.

Snow, 2005, 63 x 49 in.

brancusi bird, 2006, 8.5 x 10.78 in.

cubist SX-70, 2009, 8.5 x 10.78 in.

Praia Piquinia 29/08/08 12h11, 43 x 36 in.

Praia Piquinia 06/08/04 15h40, 43 x 36 in.

Still Water, 2010, 16 x 16 in.

Believe, 2009, 16 x 16 in.

Cari, 2010, 15 x 15 in.

Deedra, 2010, 15 x 15 in.

Burnt, 2008, 24 x 30 in.

Constellation, 2008, 24 x 30 in.

Untitled, 2010, 40 x 50 in.

Pink Grill, 2009, 20 x 24 in.

Gray chair (Single User Multiples), 2010, 4 x 3 in.

Gray chair, side view (Single User Multiples), 2010, 4 x 3 in.

Barbara Mensch's Developer Tray, 2010, 28 x 24 in.

Abelardo Morell's Developer Tray, 2010, 28 x 24 in.

Treetop Awareness, 2009, 32 x 40 in.

Untitled (Price Tag), 2009, 32 x 40 in.

Geographica, August 1976, 2010, 50 x 36 in.

Geographica, December 1977, 2010, 50 x 36 in.

Look at me, 2009, 20 x 24 in.

Weighing, 2009, 20 x 24 in.

Faceplant, Virginia, 2005, 24 x 24 in.

Huddle, Nevada, 2006, 40 x 40 in.

Arrangement #2, 2010, 50 x 40 in.

Untitled, 2010, 50 x 40 in.

Madame Leblanc (Ingres and me), 2009, 20 x 24 in.

Preparation, 2010, 24 x 30 in.

Untitled (2949), 2009, 14 x 14 in.

Untitled (2135), 2009, 14 x 14 in.

PaperPlane, 2008, 29.5 x 39.5 in.

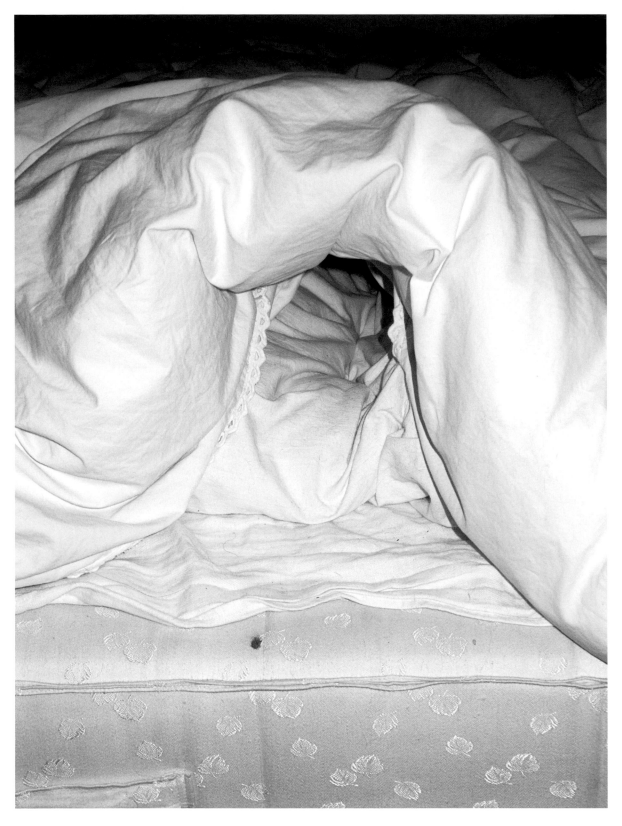

BedCave, 2007, 29.5 x 39.5 in.

Bloody Nose, 2001, 2008, 20 x 24 in.

Sistine Chapel, 2007, 44 x 54 in.

Kugach's Before for the Dance, State Tretyakov Gallery, 2009, 30 x 45 in.

Michelangelo's Moses and the Dying Slave, Pushkin Museum, 2008, 30 x 45 in.

Circle Stories #39, 2010, 50 x 40 in.

Circle Stories #28, 2010, 50 x 40 in.

A Color Notation and Interaction of Color, 2010, 16 x 20 in.

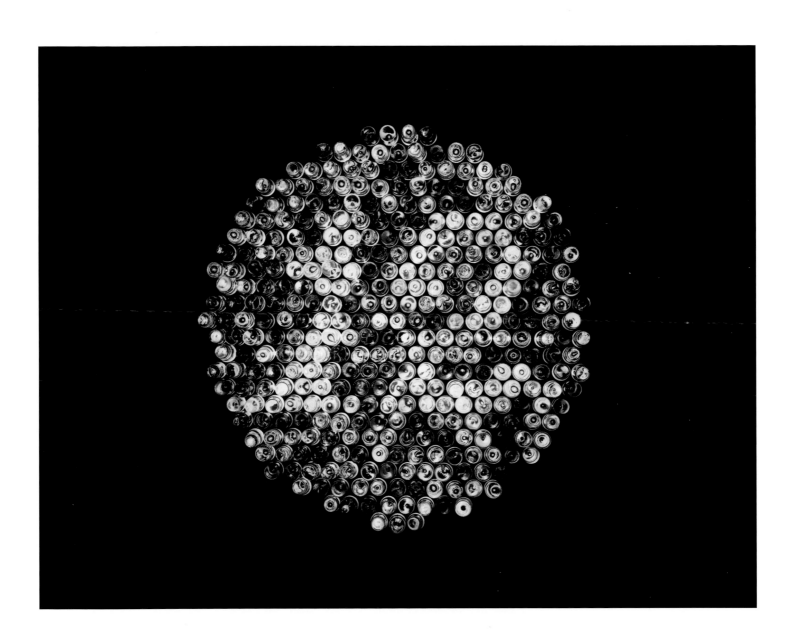

Ishihara Color Test in Lite-Brite, 2010, 16 x 20 in.

Joan of Arc, 2009, 16 x 20 in.

Cherub, 2010, 20 x 24 in.

18 possibilities, 2010, 20 x 24 in.

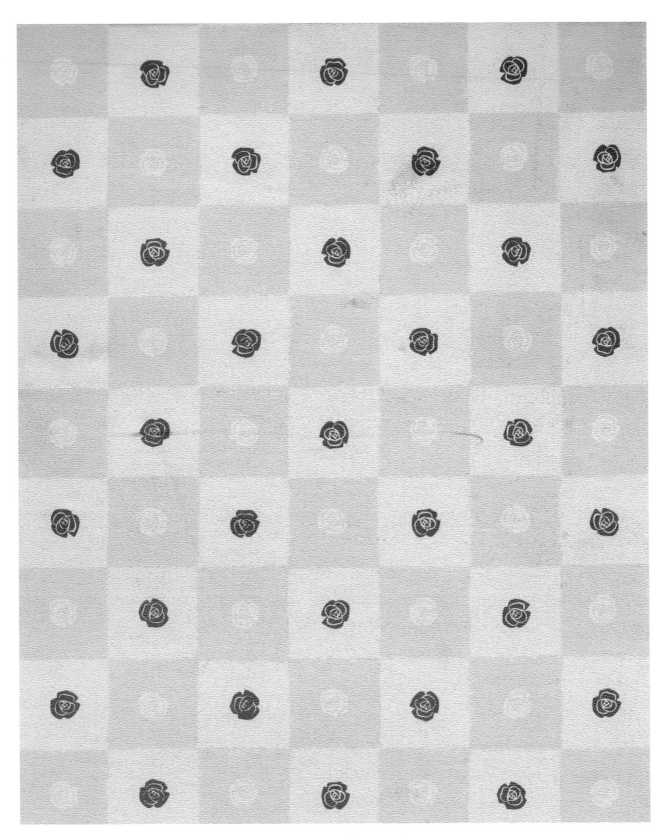

Floral-patterned yearbook cover (circa 1978), 2010, 20 x 24 in.

Dresses, 2009, 15 x 15 in.

Armchair, 2009, 15 x 15 in.

Of Augur and Auspice: No. 5, 2009, 40 x 40 in.

The Tutelary, 2010, 40 x 40 in.

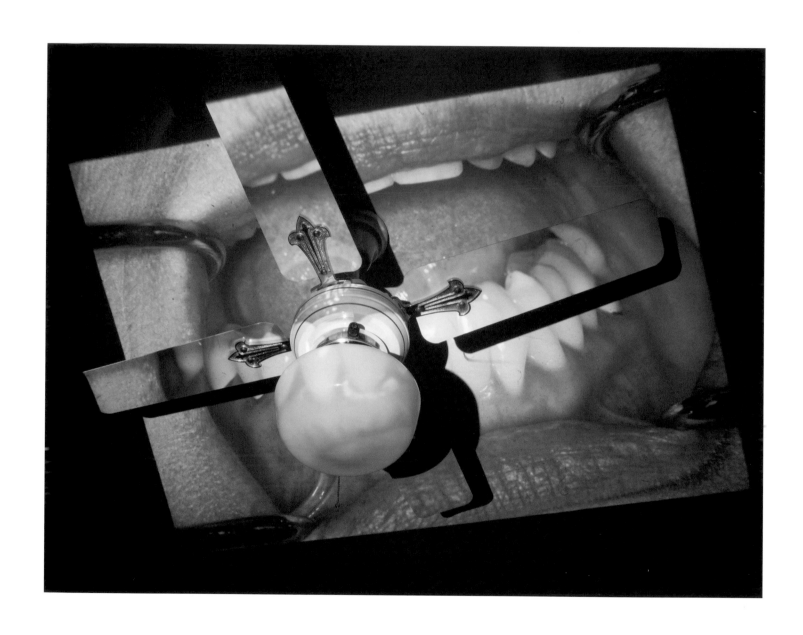

Fan, 2010, 24 x 32 in.

MAURY GORTEMILLER

Breathing Machine, 2009, 24 x 32 in.

Stillife 1, 2009, 102 x 79.5 cm.

Stillife 13, 2009, 56 x 43.5 cm.

Temple Top, Kyoto, Japan, 2005, 30 x 36 in.

Adirondack Holiday, New York, 2009, 24 x 34 in.

TNT Storage Igloo S4–A, Point Pleasant, West Virginia, 2009, 24 x 30 in.

TNT Storage Igloo S7–G, Point Pleasant, West Virginia, 2010, 24 x 30 in.

Faces, 2007, 40 x 60 in.

Untitled, 2005, 40 x 64 in.

Lagoon, 2009, 30 x 40 in.

Earth and Fog, 2009, 30 x 40 in.

Moon Studies and Star Scratches, No. 6, Saratoga Springs, New York; Middlesex, Vermont; Johnson, Vermont; Eden Mills, Vermont; Greensboro, North Carolina, June – September 2004, 40 x 50 in.

Moon Studies and Star Scratches, No. 5, Saratoga Springs, New York; Middlesex, Vermont; Johnson, Vermont; Eden Mills, Vermont; Greensboro, North Carolina, June – September 2004, 40 x 50 in.

Untitled (still from Monster Island Czar), 2010, slide projection, variable dimensions

Untitled (still from Monster Island Czar), 2010, slide projection, variable dimensions

6311–2006, 2006, 44 x 36 in.

MARTIN HYERS & WILLIAM MEBANE

6329–2006, 2006, 44 x 36 in.

Taft, 2009, 14 x 11 in.

Communist Children, 2009, 20 x 16 in.

Untitled, 2010, 16 x 24 in.

Untitled, 2009, 10 x 15 in.

Untitled, 2010, 40 x 60 in.

Untitled, 2010, 40 x 60 in.

Sweetness and Light, 2009, 12 x 15 in.

Irish Rose, 2009, 20 x 24 in.

Imitators, 2010, 24 x 20 in.

The Boarders, 2008, 50 x 40 in.

Creation, 2009, 40 x 50 cm.

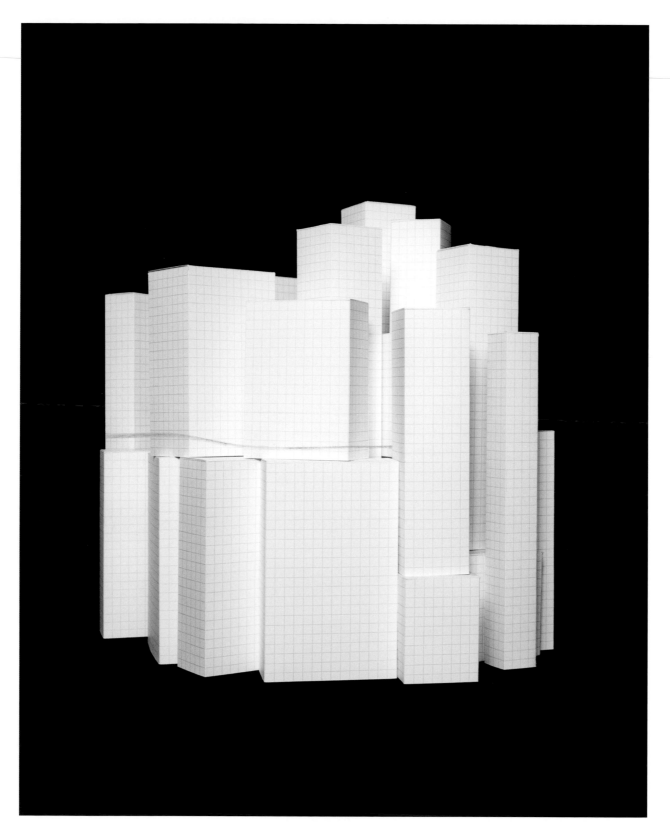

Creation, 2009, 40 x 50 cm.

Spring Migration, 2009, 36 x 28 in.

Sirpi, 2009, 36 x 28 in.

Grandpa Helping Grandma out, Mamaroneck, NY, 2000, 40 x 50 in.

Jamie Practicing for the Family, Armonk, NY, 2003, 40 x 50 in.

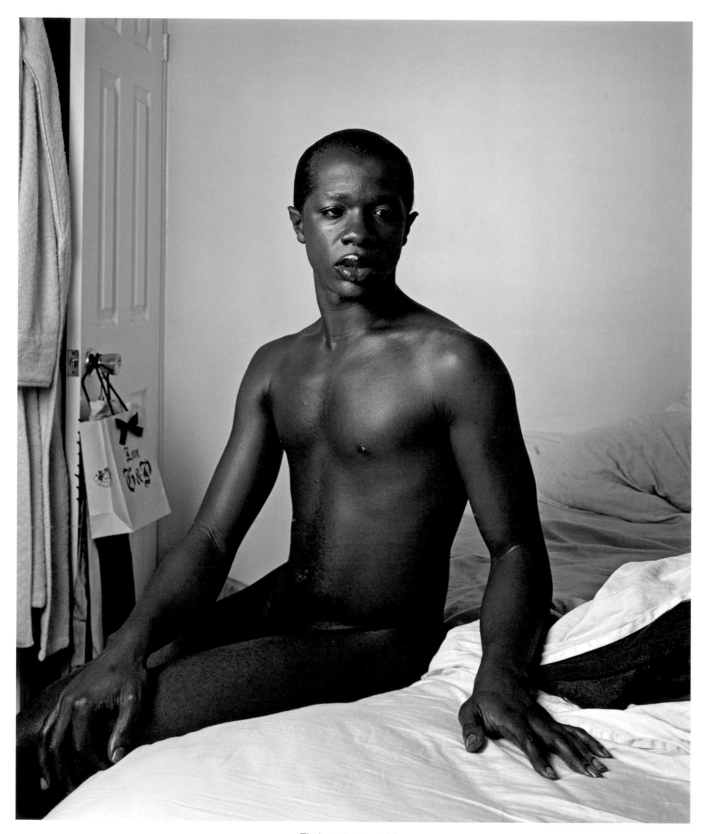

Thai, 2009, 31 x 36 in.

DEANA LAWSON

Baby Sleep, 2009, 20 x 24 in.

Curtain, Palais Garnier, Paris, France, 2009, 60 x 50 in.

Margravial Opera House, Bayreuth, Germany, 2008, 60 x 50 in.

Pat Outside of Sears, 2009, 15 x 15 in.

Woman in a Red Coat on Chestnut Street, 2009, 15 x 15 in.

ABC   WIFE SWAP   MARCH 6 2009

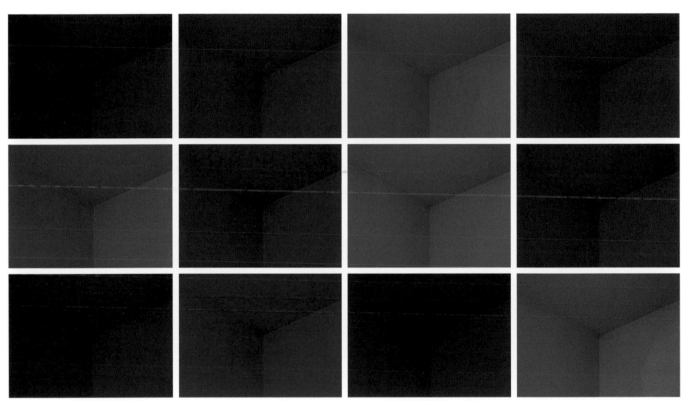

NBC   DEAL OR NO DEAL   JANUARY 9 2009

Swing, 2008, 40 x 27.5 in.

Black, 2009, 47 x 31.5 in.

Einstein Rainbow 4 (of 21), 2009, 35.5 x 24 in.

Einstein Rainbow 17 (of 21), 2009, 35.5 x 24 in.

There Are No Stars Here II, 2008, 40 x 40 in.

AVERY MCCARTHY

There Are No Stars Here III, 2008, 40 x 40 in.

Northern Cardinal, 2007, 19 x 19 in.

American Goldfinches, 2008, 19 x 19 in.

Untitled, 2009, 16 x 20 in.

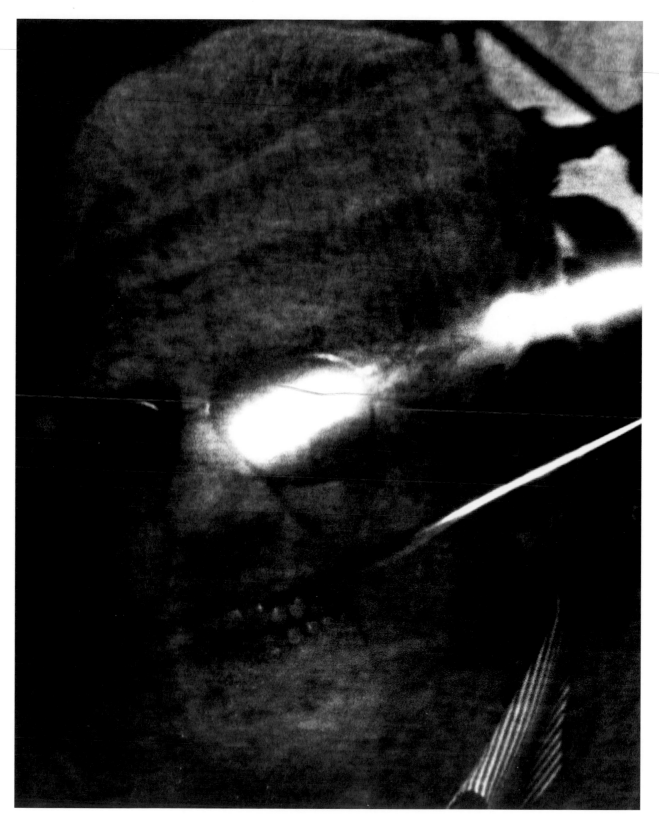

Untitled, 2009, 16 x 20 in.

My Myspace, 2010, 20 x 16 in.

Dune, 2010, 16 x 20 in.

Fish Box, 2010, 20 x 28 in.

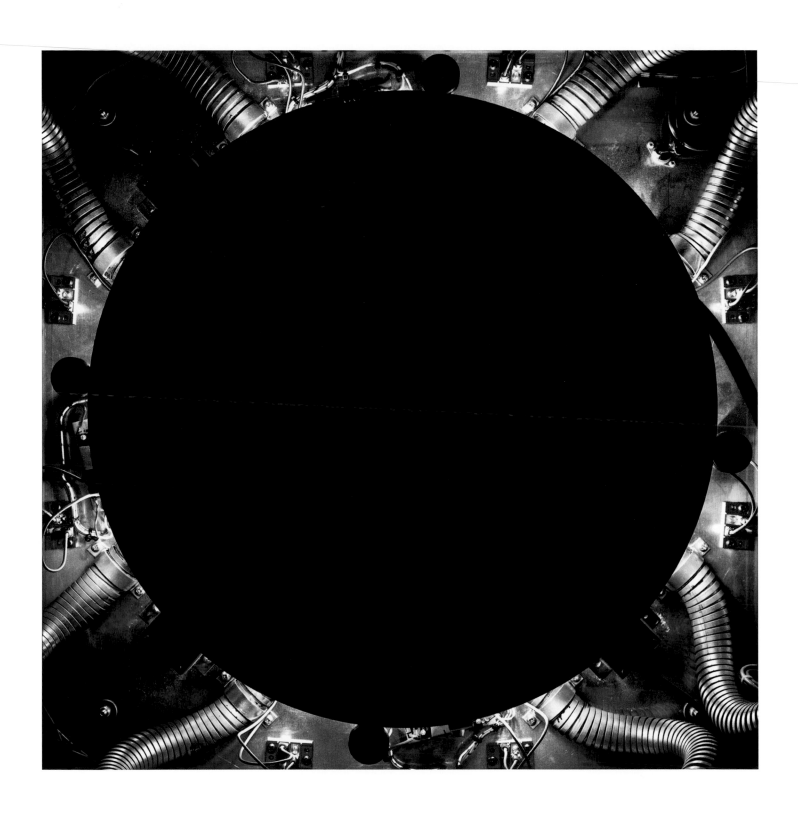

Mural Enlarger, 2008, 40 x 40 in.

Mariann, 2005, 30 x 40 in.

Sirens, 2004, 30 x 40 in.

Untitled (3D Shadow), 2007–2010, 30 x 40 in.

Untitled (Wall Drawing), 2007–2010, 30 x 40 in.

Boy with chihuahua, 2009, 8.8 x 7.5 in.

Guatemalan girl with Nana, doll and bunny, 2009, 8.8 x 7.5 in.

Seasoned Sexpot, 2009, 3 3/8 x 4 1/4 in.

MBM1594, 2010, 30 x 40 in.

08 07 26, 2008, 28 x 42 in.

08 11 25, 2008, 28 x 42 in.

I–10 Exit 159, Indio, California, 2010, 24 x 28 in.

I–8 Exit 85, Sentinel, Arizona, 2010, 24 x 28 in.

Multiplex XX, (Cinestar Cologne), 2007, 16 x 20.5 in.

Multiplex XXI, (Village–Cinemas Oberhausen), 2007, 16 x 20.5 in.

Entwine, 2008, 50 x 40 in.

Iced Over Porn, 2009, 40 x 50 in.

Untitled, 2009, 42 x 29.5 x 2 cm., LED backlight–illuminated Lambda print on Duratrans in aluminium frame

Untitled, 2009, 42 x 29.5 x 2 cm., LED backlight–illuminated Lambda print on Duratrans in aluminium frame

Untitled (from One to Nothing), 2009, 24 x 24 in.

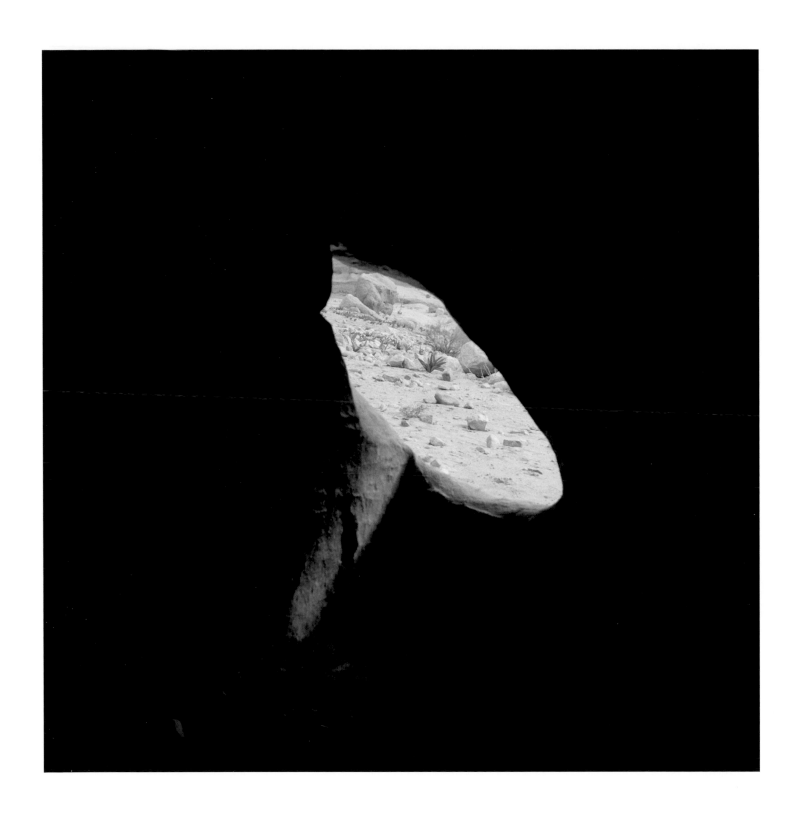

Untitled (from One to Nothing), 2009, 24 x 24 in.

Presidential Moon, 1969, 2007, 40 x 50 in.

View from the Window at Le Gras, 1826, 2009, 40 x 50 in.

Spit Shine, 2009, 16 x 19 in.

Brown Tea Party, 2009, 16 x 19 in.

Flying Hannah, 2009, 20 x 24 in.

Investigation, 2007, 30 x 40 in.

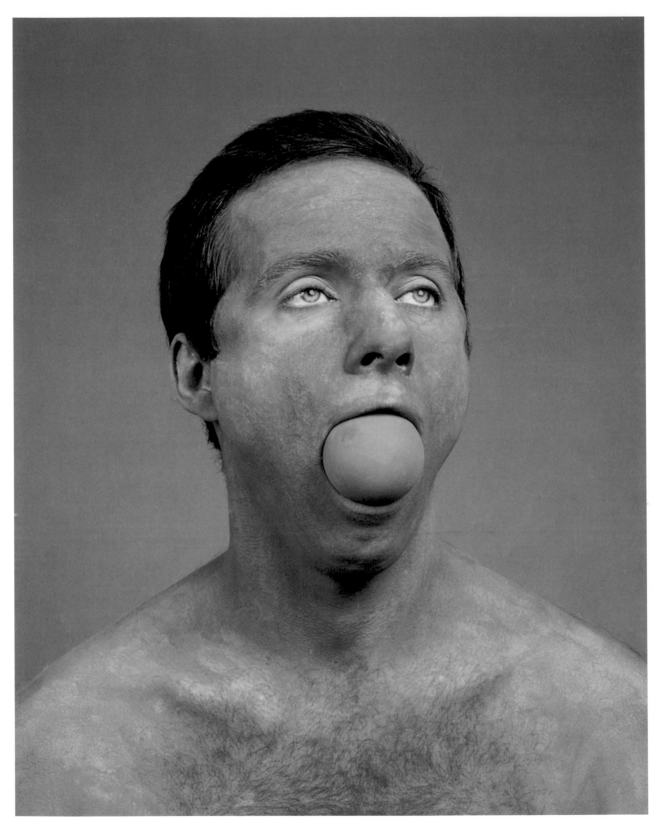

Blueballs, 2010, 40 x 30 in.

You And Your Frequent C In The Intense City, 2010, 24 x 20 in.

Kissing Trees, Rikugien Garden, Tokyo, 2009, 30 x 40 in.

Flower Box, Shimokitazawa, Tokyo, 2009, 30 x 40 in.

DETAIL, 2007, 30 x 46 in.

CREATION, 2010, 40 x 60 in.

Untitled, 2009, 20 x 24 in.

Untitled, 2009, 20 x 24 in.

Frosted Donut, 2010, 24 x 30 in.

Unsightly Bulges, 2010, 24 x 30 in.

Sunset I, 2008, 36 x 46 in.

Firefighters, 2009, 36 x 46 in.

Self Portrait with Mirror #45 II, 2008, 16 x 23 in.

Self Portrait with Mirror #60, 2009, 16 x 23 in.

New Work #38, 2009, 16 x 21 in.

New Work #43, 2009, 16 x 21 in.

Fog Field Prism, 2009, variable dimensions

Arboreal Prism, 2009, variable dimensions

Brookline, MA, 2010, 23.5 x 28.5 in.

Bloomington, IN, 2009, 23.5 x 28.5 in.

oct. 1981 E, 2006, 3.5 x 5 in.

Millee talking to Daddy WPB 1979, 2007, 3.5 x 5 in.

Sion (II), 2008, 36.2 x 43.3 in.

Rhonegletscher (I), 2007, 36.2 x 43.3 in.

After the Women of Paradise Road #2, 2010, 40 x 50 in.

After the Women of Paradise Road #4, 2010, 40 x 50 in.

Pair 2, 2007, 13 x 19 in.

Pair 3, 2010, 13 x 19 in.

Plate #11, 2010, 40 x 32 in.

Plate #82, 2010, 40 x 32 in.

Playing Card #9,, 2010, 30 x 40 in.

Playing Card #7, 2010, 30 x 40 in.

Zabriskie Point, 2009, 70 x 100 cm.

TEREZA ZELENKOVA

Cape, 2010, 50 x 70 cm.

CONTACT INFORMATION

Ketuta Alexi-Meskhishvili
Berlin, Germany
ketuta@gmail.com
ketuta.blogspot.com

Erica Allen
New York, NY
ericaallenphoto@gmail.com
ericaallenphotography.com

Ben Alper
Brooklyn, NY
(413) 320-3839
ben@benalper.com
benalper.com

Elizabeth Atterbury
Boston, MA
(207) 653-7527
elizabeth.atterbury@gmail.com
eatterbury.com
eatterbury.blogspot.com

Clint Baclawski
Boston, MA
clint@clintb.com
clintb.com

Flemming Ove Bech
Brooklyn, NY
fob@flemmingovebech.com
flemmingovebech.com

Claire Beckett
Boston, MA
info@clairebeckett.com
clairebeckett.com

　　Representation:
　　Carroll and Sons Gallery
　　450 Harrison Avenue
　　Boston, MA 02118 USA
　　(617) 482-2477
　　info@carrollandsons.net
　　carrollandsons.net

Mathieu Bernard-Reymond
Lausanne, Switzerland
info@monsieurmathieu.com
monsieurmathieu.com

　　Representation:
　　Galerie Baudoin Lebon
　　38 Rue Sainte Croix de la Bretonnerie
　　75004 Paris, France

14-1 Galerie
Galerienhaus Stuttgart
Breitscheidstrasse 48
70176 Stuttgart, Germany

Eric Bessel
Brooklyn, NY
info@besselcontemporary.com
besselcontemporary.com

　　Representation:
　　360SEE
　　1924 North Damen Avenue
　　Chicago, IL 60647
　　info@360SEEgallery.com
　　360SEEgallery.com

Magda Biernat
New York, NY
mail@magdabiernat.com
magdabiernatphotography.com

　　Representation:
　　Clic Gallery
　　424 Broome Street
　　New York, NY
　　clicgallery.com

Lucas Blalock
Brooklyn, NY
lucblalock@gmail.com
lucasblalock.com

Ryan Boatright
57 rue Hermel
75018 Paris, France
ryanboatright@me.com
ryanboatright.com

Paul Bobko
New York, NY
(917) 805-7166
paulbobko@gmail.com
paulbobko.com

Andrey Bogush
Helsinki, Finland
info@andreybogush.com
andreybogush.com

Katharina Bosse
Bielefeld, Germany
katharina@katharinabosse.com
katharinabosse.com

　　Representation:
　　Alan Koppel Gallery, Chicago
　　alankoppel@earthlink.net
　　alankoppel.com

　　Galerie Anne Barrault, Paris
　　info@galerieannebarrault.com
　　galerieannebarrault.com

　　Galerie Reckermann, Cologne
　　heidireckermann@aol.com
　　heidireckermann.com

Brian Buckley
New York, NY
(212) 946-2062
brianbuckleyphoto.com
brian@brianbuckleyphoto.com

Christian Chaize
Lyon, France
info@christianchaize.com
christianchaize.com

Elizabeth Chiles
Austin, TX
echiles@gmail.com
elizabethchiles.com

　　Representation:
　　John Cleary Gallery
　　Houston, TX

Daniel W. Coburn
Albuquerque, NM
(785) 221-0761
dan@danielwcoburn.com
danielwcoburn.com

Christopher Colville
Phoenix, AZ
chris@christophercolville.com
christophercolville.com

Helen Maurene Cooper
2704 North Whipple Street
Chicago, IL 60647
helenmaurene@hmcooper.com
hmcooper.com

Joy Drury Cox
Brooklyn, NY
joydrurycox@gmail.com
joydrurycox.com

John Cyr
Brooklyn, NY
(917) 608-2923
johncyrphotography@yahoo.com
johncyrphotography.com

Erin Desmond
Los Angeles, CA
(310) 248-0643
erin.m.desmond@gmail.com
erindesmond.com

Beatriz Díaz
Sanchez Azcona 334-201
Col. Narvarte
México, D.F. 03020
(5255) 4169 1489
bea@beatrizdiaz.com
beatrizdiaz.com

Maureen Drennan
197 18th Street
Brooklyn, NY 11215
(347) 496-9806
maureenrdrennan@gmail.com
maureendrennan.net

Amy Eckert
Minneapolis, MN
amy@amyeckertphoto.com
manufacturinghome.com
amyeckertprojects.com

Adam Ekberg
Chicago IL/Tampa FL
adam@adamekberg.com
adamekberg.com

    Representation:
    Thomas Robertello Gallery, Chicago IL
    (312) 421-1587
    thomasrobertello.com

Sam Falls
sam@samfalls.com
samfalls.com
Brooklyn, NY

Brad Farwell
Brooklyn, NY
brad@bradfarwell.com
bradfarwell.com

Maria L. Felixmüller
Leipzig, Germany
m.felixmueller@gmx.de
mariafelixmueller.de

Jill Frank
2152 West Cortez Street, Apt. 1W
Chicago, IL 60622
(917) 685-9216
jillfrank@mac.com
jillfrank.org

    Representation:
    Golden Gallery, Inc.
    816 West Newport
    Chicago, IL 60657
    info@golden-gallery.org
    golden-gallery.org

Andy Freeberg
San Francisco, CA
af@andyfreebergphotoart.com
andyfreebergphotoart.com

    Representation:
    Kopeikin Gallery, Los Angeles, CA
    (310) 559-0800
    paul@kopeikingallery.com

    Clark Galley, Boston, MA
    (781) 259-8303
    info@clarkgallery.com

Michael Gaillard
New York, NY
m@michaelgaillard.com
michaelgaillard.com

Matthew Gamber
Boston, MA
matthew@matthewgamber.com
matthewgamber.com

    Representation:
    Gallery Kayafas
    450 Harrison Avenue, No. 37
    Boston, MA 02118
    (617) 482-0411
    gallerykayafas.com
    arlette@gallerykayafas.com

Gigi Gatewood
Brooklyn, NY
gigigatewood@gmail.com
gigigatewood.com

Christopher Gianunzio
Philadelphia, PA
chrisgianunzio@gmail.com
christopher-gianunzio.com

Sarah Girner
New York, NY
sarah@sarahgirner.com
sarahgirner.com

Wendy Given
Portland, Oregon
(323) 401-9931
wendy@wendygiven.com
wendygiven.com

Maury Gortemiller
Atlanta, GA
mmgortem@yahoo.com
maurygortemiller.com

Peter Granser
Stuttgart, Germany
info@granser.de
granser.de

    Representation:
    14-1 Galerie, Stuttgart, Germany
    14-1-galerie.de

    Kaune Sudendorf, Cologne, Germany
    ks-contemporary.com

    Fifty One Fine Art Photography, Antwerp,
    Belgium
    gallery51.com

Kris Graves
3946 27th Street, Apt. 2D
Long Island City, New York, NY 11101
kg@krisgraves.com
krisgraves.com

Joshua Dudley Greer
Johnson City, Tennessee
(443) 722-9413
jdudleygreer@gmail.com
jdudleygreer.com

Matt Gunther
430 West 24th Street, #5e
New York, NY 10011
(212) 675-2694
matt@mattguntherphoto.com
mattguntherphoto.com

Stephanie Halmos
San Francisco, CA
(954) 249-2845
info@stephaniehalmos.com
stephaniehalmos.com

Sharon Harper
Harvard University
24 Quincy Street
Cambridge, MA 02138
sharonharper.harper@gmail.com
sharonharper.org

Representation:
Galerie Stefan Roepke, Cologne,
Germany, galerie-roepke.de
Rick Wester Fine Art, New York, NY
rickwesterfineart.com

Jibade-Khalil Huffman
Brooklyn, NY
khalilhuffman@gmail.com
everybook.blogspot.com
jibadekhalilhuffman.tumblr.com

Hyers + Mebane
596 Broadway, Suite 902A
New York, NY 10012
studio@hyersandmebane.com
hyersandmebane.com

Nicola Kast
Brooklyn, NY
info@nicola-kast.com
nicola-kast.com

Emily Keegin
Brooklyn, NY
(718) 757-9662
emilyelsiekeegin@gmail.com
emilykeegin.com

Ryan J. Kellman
San Francisco, CA
ryankellman@gma
il.com
ryankellman.com

Grace Kim
Brooklyn, NY
(917) 375-3152
grace@grace-kim.com
grace-kim.com

Anna Krachey
Austin, TX
akrachey@gmail.com
annakrachey.com

Jessica Labatte
Chicago, IL
jessica@jessicalabatte.com
jessicalabatte.com

Representation:
Golden Gallery, Inc.
816 West Newport
Chicago, IL 60657
info@golden-gallery.org
golden-gallery.org

Yvonne Lacet
Amsterdam, The Netherlands
yvonne@yvonnelacet.nl
yvonnelacet.nl

Representation:
Galerie Bart
Amsterdam, The Netherlands
info@galeriebart.nl
galeriebart.nl

Erika Larsen
New York, NY
e@erikalarsenphoto.com
erikalarsenphoto.com

Gillian Laub
New York, NY
glaub2@mac.com
gillianlaub.com

Representation:
Bonni Benrubi Gallery
41 East 57th Street, 13th Floor
New York, NY 10022
(212) 888-6007
bonnibenrubi.com
benrubi@bonnibenrubi.com

Deana Lawson
Brooklyn, NY
deanalawson@gmail.com
deanalawson.com

David Leventi
New York, NY
(917) 543-6410
davidleventi@yahoo.com
davidleventi.com

Representation:
Bonni Benrubi Gallery
41 East 57th Street, 13th Floor
New York, NY 10022
(212) 888-6007
bonnibenrubi.com
benrubi@bonnibenrubi.com

Arthur Roger Gallery
432 Julia Street
New Orleans, LA 70130
(504) 522-1999
arthurrogergallery.com
gallery@arthurrogergallery.com

Amy Lombard
New York, NY
amylombardphoto@yahoo.com
amylombard.com

Rita Maas
Port Chester, NY
(917) 853-3179
rita@ritamaas.com
ritamaas.com

Katarzyna Majak
Warsaw, Poland
majak@katarzynamajak.com
katarzynamajak.com
majak-desire.pl

Representation:
Zderzak Gallery
Floriańska 3, 31-019
Kraków, Poland
4812 429 67 43
zderzak@zderzak.pl

Ego Gallery
Wroclawska 19
61-838 Poznan, Poland
4861 853 15 81
ego@galeriaego.pl

Charlott Markus
Amsterdam, The Netherlands
charlottmarkus@gmail.com
charlottmarkus.com

Aspen Mays
Chicago, IL
aspen@aspenmays.com
aspenmays.com

Representation:
Golden Gallery, Inc.
816 W. Newport
Chicago, IL 60657
info@golden-gallery.org
golden-gallery.org

Avery McCarthy
Brooklyn, New York
avery.mccarthy@gmail.com
averymccarthy.com

Paula McCartney
Minneapolis, MN
paulamccartney@yahoo.com
paulamccartney.com

Representation:
KLOMPCHING Gallery
111 Front Street, Suite 206
Brooklyn, NY 11201
klompching.com

Aaron McElroy
Brooklyn, NY
(718) 902-5622
aamcelroy@gmail.com
aaron-mcelroy.com

Casey McGonagle
2257 North Sawyer Avenue, #1
Chicago, IL 60613
(323) 459-1504
casey.mcgonagle@gmail.com
caseymcgonagle.com

Jeff McLane
Los Angeles, CA
jeff@jeffmclane.com
jeffmclane.com

Monika Merva
Brooklyn, NY
(917) 279-9008
monika@monikamerva.com
monikamerva.com

Representation:
Galerie Majke Hüsstege
The Netherlands
majkehusstege.nl

Samuel Morgan
Brooklyn, NY
(917) 678-0305
sam.s.morgan@gmail.com
smorganphoto.com

Rachelle Mozman
Brooklyn, NY
rachelle@rachellemozman.com
rachellemozman.com

Tricia Lawless Murray
Los Angeles, CA
(213) 618-2827
tricia@tricialawlessmurray.com
tricialawlessmurray.com

Yamini Nayar
Brooklyn, NY
yamini@yamininayar.com
yamininayar.com

Representation:
Thomas Erben Gallery
New York, NY
thomaserben.com

Nancy Newberry
Marfa, TX
(214) 563-5603
nancy@nancynewberry.com
nancynewberry.com

Lizzy Oppenheimer
Brooklyn, NY
(310) 228-8357
lizzy@lizzyoppenheimer.com
lizzyoppenheimer.com

Georg Parthen
Berlin, Germany
info@georgparthen.de
georgparthen.de

Jennifer Ray
1441 West Albion Avenue, Apt. 3A
Chicago, IL 60626
(336) 817-1001
jennifer@jenniferray.net
jenniferray.net

Julian Röder
Berlin, Germany
mail@julianroeder.com
julianroeder.com

Irina Rozovsky
Boston, MA
irina@irinar.com
irinar.com

Adam Schreiber
Austin, TX
(646) 644-5115
adam.p.schreiber@gmail.com
adamschreiber.net

Tina Schula
38 Tompkins Place, #4
Brooklyn, NY 11231
(917) 536-7114
tinamachina.com
tinamachina@gmail.com

Robin Schwartz
Hoboken, NJ 07030
robin_schwartz@mac.com
robinschwartz.net

Representation:
M+B Gallery
612 North Almont Drive
Los Angeles CA 90069
(310) 550-0050
mbart.com

David Benjamin Sherry
Brooklyn, NY
studio@davidbenjaminsherry.com
davidbenjaminsherry.com

Emily Shur
Los Angeles, CA
emily@emilyshur.com
emilyshur.com

Mickey Smith
New York, NY
mickey@mickeysmith.com
mickeysmith.com

Representation:
Invisible-Exports
14A Orchard Street
New York, NY 10002
info@invisible-exports.com
invisible-exports.com

Kristopher Stallworth
1777 Glenwood Court
Bakersfield, CA 93306
(661) 444-9133
kcs@kstallworth.com
kstallworth.com

Kate Steciw
Brooklyn, NY
katesteciw@gmail.com
katesteciw.com

Youngsuk Suh
Davis, CA
youngssu@gmail.com
youngsuksuh.com

Bill Sullivan
42 Hudson, 5th Floor
New York, NY 10013
(646) 249-8563
billsullivanworks.com
billsullivan2@mac.com

Jordan Tate
Cincinnati, OH
jordan.tate@gmail.com
jordantate.com

Kirsten Kay Thoen
Brooklyn, NY
(718) 216-1098
kirsten@kstudionyc.net
kirstenkaythoen.com

Kevin Thrasher
Richmond, VA
kevinthrasher@gmail.com
thrasherphotography.com

Millee Tibbs
Providence, RI
millee.tibbs@gmail.com
milleetibbs.com

Corinne Vionnet
Vevey, VD
Switzerland
vionnetcorinne@gmail.com
corinnevionnet.com

Representation:
The Empty Quarter Gallery
Dubai, UAE
info@theemptyquarter.com
theemptyquarter.com

Nathaniel Ward
250 Moore Street, #101
Brooklyn, NY 11206
(917) 670-300
n.m.ward@gmail.com
natwardphoto.com

Gregory Wasserstrom
Brooklyn, NY
hello@gregwasserstrom.com
gregwasserstrom.com

Eric White
New York, NY
white@nyc.com
whiteblackwhite.com

Ann Woo
New York, NY
ann@annwoo.com
annwoo.com

Tereza Zelenkova
Opava, Czech Republic
tereza.photography@googlemail.com
terezazelenkova.com

Representation:
HotShoe Gallery
29-31 Saffron Hill
EC1N 8AV, London, UK

INDEX